COLORFAST

COLORFAST

Rose McLarney

PENGUIN POETS

PENGUIN BOOKS
An imprint of Penguin Random House LLC
penguinrandomhouse.com

Page 97 constitutes an extension of this copyright page.

LIBRARY OF CONGRESS CATALOGING-IN-PUBLICATION DATA
Names: McLarney, Rose, 1982– author.
Title: Colorfast / Rose McLarney.
Description: [New York] : Penguin Poets, 2024. | Series: Penguin poets
Identifiers: LCCN 2023027392 (print) | LCCN 2023027393 (ebook) |
ISBN 9780143137528 (paperback) | ISBN 9780593511619 (ebook)
Subjects: LCGFT: Poetry.
Classification: LCC PS3613.C5725 C65 2024 (print) |
LCC PS3613.C5725 (ebook) | DDC 811/.6—dc23/eng/20230615
LC record available at https://lccn.loc.gov/2023027392
LC ebook record available at https://lccn.loc.gov/2023027393

Printed in the United States of America
1st Printing

Set in Arno Pro with Monticello Pro
Designed by Sabrina Bowers

with love for

Elizabeth Juanita
Susan Elizabeth
Lily Elizabeth
Hannah Rose

CONTENTS

COLORFAST

Question

Such desire for the one red: the ruby.
Exceptional red, the rarity.

Not garnets, shades varied burnt to maroon.
Certainly not the ruddiness of clay

and wild plant dyes, everywhere present,
but scrubbed away, or counted as stains.

But shouldn't garnets be precious
because they are plenteous,

make finding color in the hearts of rocks
more likely? What too readily given thing

would you now kneel, in white clothes,
in ocher mud, to keep?

Sillage is the scent following after
the wearer of perfume moving through a room.

It comes from the French for a *wake,*
as in the trail left by a jet through the sky.

Once, she thought it was chopped cornstalks,
fermented and fed, in the winter, to pigs.

You can guess the kind of place she came from,
how much of anywhere she'd been. When wind

blew from the direction of the silos,
she didn't move. Would only

raise her own hand to her nose for cover,
for its soap smell, and continue whatever task

she was set to. Flight, that there was other air,
were not ideas she held then.

Realizing

"Silver seems to dominate in the Carolinian dream, when it is, of all such dreams, the one least likely to be realized." —Popular Science, 1892

Silver does dominate my Carolinian dream—recalling
granite run with metallic seams, creek beds sparkling,
glitter in graded banks and gravel roads of the mountains
I come from. My mind goes back, not to precious metal
explorers sought, but mica's shine. Mica the mineral

made into insulation for toasters and vacuum tubes,
felt, paint, roofing, joint compound. Mica the comfort
in new houses I move to, flung all across the flatness
of the map. Mica as filling in wallboard, fragments of
the Appalachian chain, linked, companions to me yet.

As when I played in old mine pits. Lowered my body
down into the ground. Lingered there, peeling layers
from solid blocks of mica called *books*. Looked through
single, translucent sheets, thin enough to admit a little
light, but not to give a clear view. My vision didn't reach

to India, Brazil, sites of more successful mines, where
mica spangles wrecked land and the lungs of its people.
Seeing far, or ahead, is difficult still. The original lens,
material from home soil, confers both focus and blur.
The page is already written when first lifted to the eye.

Spices were currency once.
Rent paid in peppercorns.

Can my dishes, so curried they amber the plates
with stains after, ensure the guests I serve stay?

No, you feed guests so they may have strength
to continue the journey away.

A good mother feeds a child so she'll grow
large, too large for the house and leave.

This was, of course, the aim of cinnamon-
toast-scented school mornings.

In the middle ages, cinnamon masked the smell
of decaying flesh. Egyptians embalmed with the spice.

What comfort is the form when it does not hold
its habitant? I would say that,

except I know when we want to care for a person,
what's available is the body.

I want to make meals for my mother now,
but she feels full always, eats nothing.

We await the results of her tests,
scans for a mass in the belly.

Nutmeg is made of the durable seed
of *Myristica fragrans*, mace from lacy red

fibers in the surrounding flesh.
Mace is worth more.

Noting the price difference, a Dutch trader,
who had never seen the plantations

of his distant colonies, sent orders:
Cut down all the nutmeg trees,

to make room for mace. He did not know.
Two spices come from the same tree.

—❧—

Two spices, one tree: an analogy.
About how the fineness of life

cannot be uncoupled from its finitude?
A French serf's life had measured value:

A pound of pepper
could buy her freedom. It is freedom

I should think of, not keeping.
Rent paid does not make a place yours

permanently. Currency has always been
intended to leave the hands in the end.

—❧—

In the beginning, my mother
held the spoon that fed me.

Hers are the hands that seasoned
the first of every of my tastes.

Later, when she'd taught me
to ladle myself full of food, she let go.

She was behaving as she was supposed to.
How can a child manage what, sooner

or later (after pause, dawdling, delay),
I must do?

Practice

Tell the fruit trees when the owner dies,
folk wisdom advises.

    To go look up into limbs, muscular
    and weight-bearing,

    or where they've been broken, marked
    by scars in the shape of eyes—

    To face their mouthlessness and try
    to work your maw,

    with which you are supposed to
    to tell others the news—

    And then figure how to want to continue
    to breathe—

This practice
is not for the sake of the trees.

All the Elizabeths

—*after North Carolina folklore*

Hold a dumb supper. Set the table in silence,
with your eyes shut, while walking backward.
If a traveler arrives in time for the meal, he
will be the one who asks you to marry him.
Girls once played this game of divination.

They were inheritors of this folk wisdom:
Boil an egg, remove the yolk, pack the hole
solid with salt, eat it, and go to bed without
drinking. If you can sleep, that thirsty, then
your groom will come to you in your dreams.

Or, they got taught justifications for
what could happen to them such as,
If you dream of a wedding, you will die soon.

> But, if a woman, in her reality, wed,
> maybe, in another dream, a girl lives yet,
>
> answering to the middle name on earth
> displaced by a husband's patronym, his claim.
> She dwells in a household of other daughters,
> so many Elizabeths, Lynns, Anns, Sues, Jos.
> Their mothers must be there, and ageless too.
>
> They pour each other tea, stir honey into
> every cup. Serve only eggs' citrine cores,
> tossing the whites to black snakes sunning
> on the porch. At night, clear the table
> of knives, dangers a hand might encounter,
>
> groping in the dark. But before that,
> they sit circled around, saying what was

unsaid at those dumb suppers, and years
more of meals, after a man's single question,
if a girl did reply *yes*.

It was pie pans, pinwheels, and strips of silver foil
when she was young. Suspending them in trees

to frighten animals from the family's fruit.
The radio playing ceaselessly its love songs

to drive off the deer if they came near the corn.
It was her mother tying tomatoes to their cages,

staking lilies as their blooms grew large, training
morning glory vines to hold to the fences. She tuned

to the romantic crooners to laugh at their absurdity.
For a time, everything kept away.

It was the mother's garden path the daughter walked
her wedding day. Through an acre solid with flowers.

Though the mother, as she always did, said the roses
had yet to reach their peak. As surely as, years after

the marriage, she'll repeat, *You should come back.*
As every summer, the daughter will do, leaving

whatever other part of the world she's been shown
and become known to, so early her husband

is sleeping, and the season more truly spring.
She'll get home before the berries are ready.

To help her mother spread bird netting. That cover,
a veil still within their power to restore.

After Viewing an Antique Blanket from My Home State, I Make the Latest Bed

—after a handwoven textile, 19th century, North Carolina, unattributed, and the spandrel depicting Ahaz, Hezekiah, and his mother, 1510, Italy, Michelangelo

It's nice to believe the past survives in sepia tones, subtle and quiet.
Many people preferred the Sistine Chapel's frescoes prior to restoration,
revelation, under centuries' layers of dirt and soot, of the original palette.

Now scenes of myth and Genesis thunder and blare in the sanctuary, garish
as a mortal's taste. On that Italian ceiling, among Christ's ancestors, some
mother wears a dress so green, shawl so purple, viewers must note its fall

from her shoulder's flesh. And the unnamed woman, back in an American
hollow, who wove the textile seen today, all woolen, tan, natural, neutral—
likely, she threw an ax head in the dye pot with onionskins and fleabane.

Hoping iron would bind brighter pigment to the piece, which was her wrap,
or better cover its stains, because it was her bedding. Her cheeks blazing
as she prodded fire. Old dyes have always run, bled, transferred (moving on

to new threads and fabric's margins). They appear faded because they were
responsive to the vividness of sun. The *before* (even the one you think your
short memory can return to, rest in, with a misty young man) when no color,

voice, or temper was high—nobody, while living, has ever been there.

Her Own

Floral complicated by chypre,
fresh mixed with musk—
the word for such a blend

of oils is *accord*.
Like a treaty signed by
a former sovereign. Soon,

she will be bent over
a store's vials of samples,
learning new terms.

Because a man
will say she must
have a signature scent,

meaning not her own skin's.
Soliflores are perfumes
featuring a single flower—

only the lily, or only
the rose. Blossoms familiar
from the garden at home,

so lush, leafy, she isn't ready
for how stripped she'll feel
in another's room. But soon,

she'll be standing up
at the finger-marked
glass and mirror counter.

It will be to old *pure notes*
she is saying *no*.

To the Hunter of Ginseng

Do not look on north slopes. Do not look in moist forests,
under broad leaves' shade. This is how you would find it,

and should you find it? Ginseng can be over-gathered. Taught
not to grow in the place it is hunted. Or killed back where it was

thickest and best. Reconsider searching for trillium, Solomon's seal,
Jack-in-the-Pulpit—the *companion plants*. A man may seek a woman's

hand like a palmate leaf. And he will receive it. But you do not have to
go there, to those north slopes. Think on the seasons ahead, how it feels

to be still pursuing the scarlet fruit. How much more do you want
of the dug-up root, the actual little body shape, shriveled and bare?

Silences

Studying the silences is what it is called
to try to discern history through recipes.

Which is to take measure of the scant
documentation of some information, while

remembering kitchens have always been loud
with lids banging on pots come to boil, bursts

of bubbling oil, knives' clash and cleave,
talk of meat and bread, curing and uprising.

Those who did the cooking didn't get
to darken white pages with their writing.

They were kept busy sinking fish fillets
into the pallor of bowls of milk, soaking

them to make the aftertaste mild, serving
them with the eyes cooked blank and leaves

of lettuce laid over the heads. Still, the lips
beneath, fried open wide, had plenty to say.

As a girl,

an empty homestead, set way back
from any road, was where I liked to go.

House with a swing fallen to the porch floor,
stopped pendulum for measuring a time past.

Pipes that had summoned
spring water become just scattered lines

lying in the high grass. The distant kin
of the last old lady to die

in this place could get no use
of the cookstove, wood-burning as it was,

or the worn furniture left to become
campers' kindling. They took this

final care of the house: propping all the doors
open. Saying, there is nothing of value.

There is no need troubling to break in.
Still, I would stay at the edge of what had been

the scythed clearing. Whisper if I spoke.
Not take so much as a canning jar holding

only the lavender discoloration of years
with its own glass. Never cross a sill.

Because I had seen the daylilies
and knew a woman must have set them,

and peered out at the night's darkening,
and that if she lived

here, in a woman's skin, it was in
fear of rough entry.

                           Boys played
elsewhere, at the construction sites

of subdivisions. Running, shouting,
through the new houses' scaffolding,

not caring about walls. Not waiting
for their completion to mount

the risers of stairs, or questioning
whether offices and master bedrooms

would be theirs.

He'd pass notes I had to hide
(stolen answer keys to tests
I didn't ask to see),

pull out my chair, sliding
his hands down my sleeves.
Of course, I stayed quiet.

He'd miss school for days
and say only that his mother
had slept too late to drive him.

Of course, the dark circling
one eye or another of hers wasn't
the shade of the well-rested.

(His words, to be particular
about it, were, *Lazy bitch
won't get out of bed.*)

But there are matters to be kept
at home, given privacy.
The class bought an alarm clock

for the family, plastic hands
to intercede. I hadn't thought
of him, the ticking,

for thirty years. Until hearing
the news that he'd blown off
his own hands, building a bomb.

And local women murmuring,
*He's not a terrorist. It was only
his daddy he meant to kill.*

At least he isn't the kind
to target a public place.
These ventured beneath

the general *Beats me*
or *No comment* at all.
Yes, we'd gone to school,

been folded into desks'
narrow holds, alongside him.
We'd learned rules, like

keeping our hands to ourselves.
A few things we do know.

Remains

Burning fuel but not to travel away,
boys cruised circles around town. Then,
came back, to park at the gas station
where they began. Girls stayed in the lot.
Waiting for men with powers endowed

by time. Strangers of age to buy liquor
would do for a while, until the local boys
grew up enough, got ready to realize claims
on the land where, already, roads, schools,
and cemeteries bore their names. So we

could take, or be taken by them, too.
It seemed our staying, boys' circling, were
the continuation of all that was ever done.
We didn't consider the figure standing
across the street, as it had for a millennium:

the mound, built by people preceding
the Cherokee. Where the townhouse
of that ancient civilization would have been.
What might be lying beneath. Or legends
of sacred fire buried and still blazing there.

Neither did we yet know what the town founded
this century had interred—oil tanks. Which leaked.
While we struck matches, dropped cigarettes, and
watched boys' hands at rest on the steering wheels
of leased trucks, eager for their next move, fingers

of combustible seepage reached in the direction
of the mound. Yet we were spared flames. Allowed
to go on, speaking of *we* (unaware of all it didn't hold),
a little farther into what young history we'd heard,
loitering on the surface of that earth.

Giving It Thought

When I first heard the term *invasives* referring
   to plants in the woods, foreign varieties choking out
      some native ground covers and shrubs, it sounded
         like a mean-spirited name. Is it fair to blame those
            who are taller and stronger and so surer to succeed?

Then the extermination of pythons—because they strangle,
   swallow birds, rabbits, the bobcats that were the predators,
      every living thing—in another state's swampy landscape
         raised the question of who gets to determine which parts
            of nature are to be preserved, or deserve disciplining.

And measures taken—strapping a tracking device to the back
   of a male, to follow to burrows where females hide, to shoot
      them inside—seemed sad for all involved. It's true, he's let go,
         continues to be the end to many mates. But he couldn't know
            what he was doing. Surely not, and with intention, do it again.

Now, in the public park of my own town, I stand
   under monkey bars and vultures flapping burger wrappers,
      eyeing, amid the litter, torn satin panties. With handprints
         circling in the dirt. Assuming the marks are less likely clues
            of force used than of the positions desire takes. A woman,

and these the thoughts I give in to.

Language that goes around
the edge of the land, describing
distances and directions between

markers to connect in a line—
that's what the metes and bounds
method of surveying provides.

It relies on a stand of pines, a bend
in the creek, a fence's far corner—
references of that kind. *It's an art,*

says the man in the courthouse office
shaking his head at the wordy papers
that define a woman's property.

She's dressed up—ironed, tucked in—
to come with concerns: a trespasser,
showing ownership, where her side is.

The man puts it that way to get at
the subjectivity. Trees can fall prey
to beetles. Streams are shifty, swayed

by slight suggestions of topography.
As a reminder that not all evidence
can be depended upon. People talk

this way who would prefer the earth
parceled out in standard lots. Will buy
only what's square, confirmed, clear.

They say *art* with as much love of art
as when they say a woman *embellishes*
wept claims. But I'm just here listening

as I wait to pay taxes today. If some
emotion smears my face's features,
it's not surprise. I'm not so naive I believe

a few split rails are enough to ensure
any boundary. I do know how likely
a blouse's buttons are to be undone.

Meditation on a Faded Dress, and What Can Be Done

Dye—to impart color, sometimes permanent.
   The permanency already muddled equivocal by
      the adjective. *Adjective*, in dyeing terms, refers
         to color applied only on the surface, not fixed
            deep in the fibers. Adjectives are words such as
               rosy, pretty, descriptors or modifiers of what is
                  substantive, creating states like *maybe, formerly.*

And *dye* is a verb, an action, motion, change.
   And a *homophone* that sounds like what comes
      after the final gesture, or shudder, is made.
         A doubleness meaning that everything is
            through. What, did you think you would be
               permitted more possibilities in the end?

How Well They Liked the Meal

Baste meat throughout the day,
after searing, before deglazing.

Between, break beans, devoting all
your fingers to each small shell.

Crimp crust, pare and slice fruit thin.
Keep chopping; a single forkful

shovels up so many juliennes. Know,
no matter how well the table is laid,

soon the fed stand, wiping their hands.
Be ready to do dishes, twirling a rag

around tines and rims before remains
of the meal can harden. Think of

the ballet, a display of perfected bodies.
Which the audience must leave

at the show's end. This does not mean
they do not understand the dance,

live as it was, was danced
tonight's particular way once only.

Let the dinner be eaten.
Then breakfast, and lunch again.

Prepare the kitchen for tomorrow.
By the time you are through,

the theater will be unoccupied, except,
perhaps, by an individual glove.

It offers some applause—
the quiet half of clapping,

when palms fall apart, open.
That the plates be emptied—

was that not your ambition?

Receipts

We tried out different endings for ourselves,

scribbling *Mrs.* plus the last name
of whoever was kicking the cloud of dust obscuring
the ball that was the object of his game.

The girls in my class bent over
our notebooks, under the playground oaks.

⮞

Mary Maddison was a girl in the 17th century, known
because she practiced her name again and again
in a historic manuscript. (*Of historical significance*
not said of any girl's efforts until
long after she is gone, of course.)

Many times, introducing *Mary,*
she first set in writing, *I am.*

⮞

I remember not liking my married names much.

But we had gotten the idea
we should be given away,

and wipe out how we had been called,
the titles we'd labored to make clear
in chalk letters on the board.

⮞

The kitchen is where girls
in the 1600s, in England, learned.
From listening to talking women, watching
the math of measuring, and copying
receipts, recipes.

Mary's manuscript was the margins
of a cookbook—the paper available to her.

⁓

After a time, my school's oaks
were cut down because of the danger
they could fall. Too much wildness.

Then too little shade. Girls began
to pass lunchtimes inside, doing homework.

This was good practice for skipping meals entirely,
which some among us would come to do.

⁓

Strawberries, raspberries, script scrolls large
above centuries-old recipes, repeating.

Though script is not quite
what the crooked figures are.

This is the writing of a beginner.
To continue, she had to believe in a goodness
that hadn't happened yet.

⁓

A girl is given a basket, play eggs
of heavy wood to load it. Also, dresses
for dress-up with sashes, to wrap the waist
tight in satin.

A recipe is a proposition that what will follow,
if you follow the steps, will be as promised
in the title from the beginning.

A girl wishes to be a woman. Then a woman
wishes to look girlish (what stays slim
is the chance of this).

—❧—

After a time, Mary—penmanship improved—reproduced
a poem about birds flying away. An instructional poem
for women, for *when your beauties end.*

Had she progressed to baking cakes by then?

—❧—

Cursive isn't taught at school anymore. I hardly remember
it myself. Such a scrawler I've turned into.

A signature that seems barely composed of the alphabet:
Is the carelessness a sign of one who
does not need to prove that she's able?

Or who does not want to be too visible?

—❧—

Do I overlook the opportunity
to study the imperatives in recipes?

Pound, peel, slice,
scald, stir, skewer:

Is a cook not given examples
of how to speak commands?

—❧—

The items in an ingredient list are assumed to have some relation
to each other by dint of their adjacency in procedure,
the linguist argues.

Sugar follows butter because they become creamed together.

I stood by women of my family as they cooked the yields
of whole orchards down into canning jars.

—❦—

From the many possible messages
in the aforementioned, some will take
the one of strength.

Some will make sweets for others,
but not eat them.

Some were proud, once, to be able
to write out precise recipes,
to pass on mastered words.

—❦—

Did Mary ever have a chance to offer
directions written in her own hand
to a friend, ever have enough free paper?

Perhaps I should have taken pride
in my wild childhood Ys and Ts,
that shot out extra branches,
like trees.

—❦—

So often, recipes end with a phrase such as *serves four*
or *salt to taste*—a coda.

What happens after the writing ends
and dinners begin? Do the women I once called
friends, or *Dawn* or *Donna* or *Darlene* or *Misty*,
fill their plates this evening?

Or do they keep busy passing dishes, then
washing off any print of their fingers, whatever
grease they leave? What was it that we shared?

—*with gratitude for* Eat My Words: Reading Women's Lives through
the Cookbooks They Wrote *by Janet Theophano and* "Claiming a Piece
of the Pie: How the Language of Recipes Defines Community" *by Colleen
Cotter*

Blackberries

When summer is full,
the sparrows are too.

So overfed on berries
they cannot fly. You've seen

them in the road,
bodies extruding fruit,

run over. There long after
the minutes of glut. Still

you put by berry jelly.
As though *preserve*

were really the word
for anything you can do.

Or winters of any sort
will be deterred by your jars

perching at shelves' edges,
glass bellies bulging, dark.

When Temperatures Fall

Snow melts from around the oaks before disappearing
from the field. Departs sooner from shade and shelter.

Isolate stretches of white where the land's been cleared—
unlikely sites of forbearance—may suggest lingering

chances for others too. But it is just that trees hold heat
absorbed from the sun, slow-release what was gathered.

The thaw is caused by their loss—greater every hour.
On night's far side lies sunrise. That's when temperatures

fall. Light, when it shows, makes small difference to how
the air feels then. What matters is warmth trunks and limbs

stored over the longer course. They have given all, are spent
by morning. Which comes icy, slippery, under the treads

of the old woman, bent into the cold. Now there is nothing
her children (not children any longer) can do. It is her will

to go out walking in weather like this, bones of her shoulders
tensed ahead.

Crepuscular

It was months I'd been running that way,
months before first snowfall. Then I saw
the prints. Not a dog; there were no claws.

None in the tracks, I mean. A feline walks,
those powers withdrawn into her toes.
It was cougar paw, cougar paw.

How many days had I been seen, how many
in surplus granted me, by what lenience
was I let to continue,

breathing heavily as the miles accrued?
Then I saw prints every morning, laid
also with each new snow. I kept on

running there at dawn. This was the winter
of wondering, not at the evergreens,
their dense cover, their vigor,

but if I had to survive my mother, how much
grief I'd have to have, and get relieved, to be
forgiven for an action that brought it to her.

Crepuscular, instead of *dawn,*
is what I called that low-lit hour,
(screeching, spit-sounding word

that doesn't care whether
it speaks of sun or evening coming)
and let the cougar decide—

That winter passed, and I moved through
the months. To see *Puma concolor* declared
extinct from my side of the country.

I missed the flash of gold fur coursing
through pale iced trees, and what more
that my color vision should have perceived?

Still, at least twice, I was let to have a life,
and after its givers, alone will endure.

I've been economical
in hotels. Done laundry
in sinks. Let phones
lie at rest. (What to say
if I did dial?) Behaved
like the daughter of people
I love. (Though they'd save
such a word as well.)

In far cities, waiting
for sleep, I've heard
compliments called
down halls, exchanged by
strangers to me. But who
seem to be everyplace,
recognizing every night as
an occasion to dress up for.

Seen a dry cleaner's order
form (that I left blank,
of course) turn warning:
*Objects left in pockets will not
be returned. The condition of
buttons, elastic, trim, and sequins
is not guaranteed. Brighter
colors may not hold fast.*

And had to feel even a litany
so mercenary was readier
to name what's dear
—what's loss is feared—
than the most poetic
elegy. Which will always
be too late, speaking of
what has passed.

Though Not Yet Forty, I Wrote

The rot smell rising from the sewer: It must be the fox, dead.
   Once, the point of her head, night-seeing eyes, below ground-
smelling nose, led the narrow line of her body, a nib inscribing
   the vague gray of the neighborhood with red. This was before

mange removed her coat. Before she exposed herself further
   in the middle of afternoons and streets. Before she fell rolling,
wishing for her own skinning, to get free of the itch, the burn,
   that living in the flesh had turned. Now look back earlier still,

to the house where a girl spoke her first sentence: *It was fox.*
   At the window, gesturing toward trees it had paused between.
She continued the exclamation through the seasons. The same
   no matter the time passed since, or how the after kept growing.

From the start, choosing past tense. Even in her first home,
   circled by her mother's gardens and fields, and those held in
a ring of forest's greater green. Before she ever left and saw
   places lowly as this late fox's den, or familiar ground asphalt-

interred, she was conjugating toward a point beyond earth.
   Already speaking of remembrance, beginning the one thing I,
with my volumes of sad words that save nothing, can stay—
   which is true to who I have always been.

As she died, as she was
fossilized, the ichthyosaur
had her three young alongside.

One pushed out first
to flap in the rough sand alone.
One in the birth canal,

the last in line, pinned behind,
who'd take no breath of its own.
And one dangling,

head extended into the world
where the body couldn't follow,
beak and eye agape.

The mother had no choice
about whether hers was a part
of history to bring life into.

She couldn't have carried
knowledge their kind would soon be
extinct or the burden of supposing

it was just as well this way, or taken
blame for acting too early or late.
The sediment came when it did,

sealing them in their varied positions,
their shared impression in stone.
The one caught in-between

looks hungry for whatever will
fit into its minutes. Its pupil
is directed right at me. Or, rather,

the opening once filled
by another eye, where now
there's the absence of even

the outlines left by bone, a socket
with nothing to hold.

Every summer that I was a child,
there were kittens. There were
eyes to watch, opening baby blue,
widening, and turning to yellow
like the fields. It would be fall then,
time for new homes, and repetition
of the evening when my mother
surrendered to tears, more wracked
with practice, never more prepared

for loss, as the cars taking kittens,
and another season, moved on.
Even the cats we said we'd keep
were truck-struck and dog-shaken,
or, in spite of spoon-feeding,
wounded feet dressed in booties,
disappeared, fading into the edges
of forest and day, those greater
quiets and calicos. The end

of every short life of theirs
breaking up the blousier span
of human years. Though
there were also the times when
cats we thought were missing
were found sleeping, stretched
in the sun, in the suggestion
of things longer than summer
or its shadows. Such as lineages

of all the litters ever bred.
And couldn't the stripes
of all the tabbies, untwined,
turn out to be a single string?

This isn't childish thinking.
It's later when a person needs
to believe in some thin, silken,
and unseverable thread.

Animals never choose to end their lives because they cannot imagine
narratives, and so cannot dread how they will continue, scientists say.
Only those who can conceive of a future can want to give up a part in it.

So whales beaching themselves by the dozens, *sick leader hypothesis*
explains, are following the lone one among them with orientation altered
by illness, not their wish. We school around my grandfather's cot where,

despite damage no surgery can repair, age, so many reasons, he does not
die. He stays. His hand swelled to illiterate claw, tongue un-obeying, but
all he needs is to say, *Susie, Sandra, Lily*, or *Rose*, it doesn't matter which.

One of his girls, daughter or child born of her, any member of the group
will behave as the rest. We are all still standing here. It will take suffering
weeks of the strongest arguments to convince him of what lies ahead,

while we, the view at his feet, appear as if we wish to go on living.
And answer to, try to follow the direction of, whatever cry he issues.

A waterfall impedes travel, and a mountain slows.
A straight-line measure of mileage between points tells
little of how a walker really moved over land's features.

We are unable to fly. What humans can choose is not
to cross streams or ridges in a straight shot, though
the distance would be lesser if swum or clambered.

Usually, we've gone around, on the route at a hill's feet,
or that kept our own dry. Followed *least-cost pathways*—
archaeologists' term referring to where past pedestrians,

accounting for terrain, are likeliest to have stepped.
What is *cost*? In 1000 AD, perhaps the people
who lived here preferred length of effort to force.

Perhaps time rather than exertion was the currency
with which they, with their trails winding slow
and level through the valleys and meadows, paid.

What is *we*? Settlers who spoke of taking
the long, crooked road, migrating to the mountains,
are the lineage I can come nearest to claiming.

They picked dirt so rocky it bent tools, wouldn't yield
food. And stayed, as if to choose dramatic scenery
was to set beauty as the highest value. But hard labor

is as central to their story. In which some estimation
of profit led to plowing sacred Native mounds,
in a few generations wearing them down to half

the height they'd been for a thousand years.
To displacements more terrible still. And to me,
learning to take my first steps on disturbed ground,

then pocketing pottery shards I found. To encounter
again later, opening boxes of childhood collections
and questions about *my* and *first*, *acquire* and *know*.

⇝

At home, like anywhere, cheaper has come to mean
the closest spot for constructing the parking lot.
Ease, bulldozers filling streams and wetlands,

laying mounds and mountains low. And, over paved
plateaus spreading out around chain stores, I've rolled
a rattling cart holding whatever purchase I could afford.

Though I also spend evenings tracing connections
between ancient sites on archaeologists' maps of my
home county. Studying their conjectures of the hours

a Mississippian would have to have given
to walk to each village from the town center.
Figuring in which places it had cost more

than a day's time to arrive. I picture dwelling
uphill, upriver, where others might tire before
reaching to deliver hard news, at a remove that far.

The Collectors of Local Minerals Are
Likelier to Find What They Seek

From the land comes corundum.
Called that, or ruby—

the mineral is the same.
The difference is the grade given

by an appraiser. He gets to say
what isn't a gem, will be a fortune.

A girl from this place
may be chosen

to play tinsel-haloed Mary
in the church pageant or

as another member of the choir.
To become the rhinestone-tiaraed

homecoming queen or
a wife whose roots grow out

from the platinum dye
while waiting on a man's return,

for him to remember the vows
he's bound by.

Why wouldn't she stay?
What would she do

but wear that dark crown
of hair the color intended for her?

She doesn't need to go off
after diamonds, or to study

some other distinction, knowing,
with certainty, there are plenty

of rocks in the dirt here.
She's familiar with hymns and He

who determines beginnings, judges
to the end. Always, she sings praise.

From the section *How the Twig Should Be Bent* comes
this advice about rooms for sons: *Create an atmosphere
of freedom where there are few, if any, don'ts. Translate
your ideas into masculine colors, fabrics, and furniture
that will withstand even unreasonable wear and tear.*

Rooms for daughters should manage girls' desire
for change, their impulse to redo space allotted
to them: *Temporary expressions ought to be recognized
as such and made easily convertible to another style.*

The lady is to devote herself to room templates, sketching
doors, radiators, a house's set fixtures. Then trace, clip,
and move settees, davenports, sideboards—possibilities.

I write, my material is paper, like the grandmother
who left this book with pages of draft arrangements
for furniture. I am inheritor of pieces my grandfather

rendered real with his purchase, such as what he
referred to as her dressing table. I tried it place after
place before positioning it in my study. In good light
where I can call it a desk. On the surface where once

she set a bulb-circled mirror, leaned in to determine
what to line, to gloss to shine, to powder flat, and
blend away, I now revise, mark and erase. I sit below
the window, turning the direction potted plants train
themselves toward, the way they strain to face.

One Kind

Sleeping with her husband, palm pressed to his chest,
she is not thinking of Adam's rib, the insult of the notion
woman is but a splinter, a derivation of him. She is at rest.

Her love's ribs bow a bit outward, but he isn't pigeon-
chested. The bone is not so overgrown. It's just a little
extra protective layer. Or the cage door is propped ajar.

Say *dove-chested*, then. Most languages don't distinguish
between pigeons and doves, as English does. Both
are included in the Latin, are of the order Columbiformes.

But if he is described as a bird, surely it should be the kind
bearing an olive branch meaning peace, no matter the religion.
Suggesting everything that has happened can be gotten over

and trust dredged up again. So she lies curled, fetal, as if to crawl
back into him, go back to zygote, to yolk. Maybe she dreams
that, if he was called *keel-chested*, at least he might be a boat.

Yes, let him be an ark where a creature can shelter, stay. Refusing
to go ashore, fall under dominion, become a sacrifice, or be divided
from rider into ridden, from those with appetite into flesh eaten.

Choosing not to step out of the kingdom where all are Animalia
and there are no herds, packs, flocks to complicate matters between
mates. (No other cock to show his color, spurs, temper, features

males have in common, but that the hen doesn't share.) The woman
doesn't want to remember other men. There is more than one
reason to stay in the tight space of the hold, hunkered in our pairs.

Once, the bat used the same senses as me, before
echolocation ventured out of his head, into the dark,
and returned, reverberating, to his skull's enclosure.

Then, he evolved to be free from the need to see, smell,
or touch to perceive the positioning of things. Lost
any use for hands, features we might have shared, if time

had traveled forward differently. Uncertainties fluttered,
appended to his sides, in the beginning, possibilities
of arms that withdrew into his shoulders. After,

five phalanges remained, one stuck up and out, as a reminder
of thumbs. But the others thinned, and the pinkies, if that's what
they almost were, are evasive now, in their places at the elbows.

Membranes the bat glided on didn't shrink to the rudimentary
webs I see between my digits when spread (in the gesture
that offers my palms, empty). His skin grew instead into wings.

Once, I was told bats tangled in girls' curls. A girl can believe
others will fling themselves into being near, when their gazes
have just started to be laid on her form's unfurling. She may

not worry about why the bat extended what could have been
hands to take flight, rise beyond reach. She does not yet know
anything well enough for it to feel old, how parts of the body

can fold, or the shape of prayer. Prayer: Let this love keep
sleeping, limbs tangled in mine, even when my hair knots
around his finger, thickens his ring with more binding silver.

Hush

I am studying, finally, the pines.
Trying to hear the hush

of forest floors under needles'
cover, their soft erasure.

Not as lacking the stirring
of deciduous, varied,

and tangled understories
of shapely leaves.

But as more than
an absence of sound.

Years, the woods felt foreign
here, where I came

to teach. The students are 20,
saplings of men. A woman

can only mature beyond
where the eye wishes to reach.

When timber grows tall
it is cleared away.

Centuries already,
the longleaf pine has been

lumbered out of existence
in this place.

Still, along with loblolly,
white, pond, and sand,

late, I am learning its name.
There may never again

be occasion to say it aloud
upon seeing one.

But who knows what life
continues, in that quiet

where I will go.

Each Morning Again

As the sky darkens and window displays
are taken down—that is when she walks home,
tired. To take off her good shoes.

To her husband. What to express about
another such day? The given hand
composes shopping lists. As if reminders

were wanted, of the staples, every week the same.
(Though is it any better how produce changes,
so seasonal and fickle and wilt-prone?)

She goes home to the cat, to pet him
where he poses, always on the edge
of the room, as if considering exiting.

But the jeweled necklaces, kept safe overnight,
are lifted back into view, onto mannequins'
velvet throats, each morning again.

Bodies rise everywhere. To possibility
and could be. Poets return to making metaphors'
pairs, which must be unexpected. And the cat,

it turns out, loves this life, surprisingly much.
When he becomes ill, he struggles to, once more,
map the neighborhood by familiar odors.

Now, in the remains of earlier prey, strands
of worms shine and curl. Their time
just beginning. The eggs like pearls.

Holds Me Here

Once it seemed the world worked in opposition
to survival, to the will, the wits, the musculature,
of a head-tossing creature. Put horses in stalls
from which their vibrancy had to smash free.

Now I read about a horse saved from fire
by a swimming pool cover. It entangled, clasped,
held her back from running through a forest
in flames, from going to her own end.

Buoyed her too. She who, even having
fallen into the good fortune of water, without
the plastic's lift, could not have stayed afloat.
And it has come to seem that what conspires are,

instead of the forces that break, those that spare.
I have taken too little care, let my body blaze
with hunger's emptiness, all varieties of excess,
then, from others, turned coldly away.

These days, I shiver a dampening shake,
so hard, my own flesh might leave its bone.
Still, in this life, I remain, and my husband,
whenever I pass by, he reaches out his hand.

Heart

—*after "Observations and Experiments with Madder-Root, Which Has the Faculty of Tinging the Bones of Living Animals of a Red Colour"*

Birds who fed on crimson
madder flowers tinted
their beaks bright red.

Were they dyed
all through, so vivid
down to the marrow?

To answer the question,
they were made specimens.
Turned skeletons. Examined

like rocks split wide
to show jewels earthy
cover might hide.

Loves who have not yet left,
who are not yet so old: It's you
I think of as I learn of birds

never again to move
through air. May I not
be one for whom it takes

seeing a body reduced
to bone, broken,
to believe the beauty

it had held in.

How We Celebrated

I was celebrating when I sighed—
at the sauce reducing, the pastry nothing
but butter, the wine that wouldn't be so good
the next day. I saw the portions served to me.

If I ran from the rain, said it would ruin
the high style in which I piled my hair,
this was only to measure how far
ideas like drought were from mind.

Pacing, waiting for guests, fearing their
arrival past the flowers' freshest hour—that was
my pleasure. I knew such irritations depend on
the surety that they who are late will be here yet.

And, after parties, in our earliest years,
we played in piles of wrappings. Enough gifts
had been given to do this—to bury each other.
Presents are covered with paper, with attention

to folding the fit at the corners, tucking the edges
under. Aware of, preparing for, the tearing apart.

Cakewalk

Pound, foam, sponge, sheet, chiffon, velvet,
devil, angel, gold, lightning,
layered, jelly-rolled, spring-formed, Bundt-shaped,
petit-four-sized, liqueur-soaked, baked upside down—

so many kinds of cake.
Imagine them all ringed around one room.

And a cakewalk commencing.

How long the walk would be
if the circle were to encompass every cake
someone has sifted, separated, whisked, folded,

and fussed over to raise up something fine
on a stand, under a glass cover, no crumbs
on the frosted surface.

My elementary school held cakewalks.
People orbited the gymnasium, over
red free-throw lines, under pink crepe paper,
accompanied by fiddle, or maybe
it was a cassette tape.

If I had gotten to play, I would have
moved across that floor praying
for a very particular fate.

But my mother didn't want me to have too much
sugar, not every day. She wanted better for
her own girl. So I stood on the sidelines, apart.

I wanted the cake from Crystal's mother.
She decorated cakes at the grocery store,
obscured cakes under piles of icing,
full skirts into which she inserted
princesses' plastic torsos.

The icing was sugar whipped stiff
with lard.

Grocery shopping, just for myself this week, after
choosing sensibly (no candy, no jam),

I waited at the register,
watching a little boy.

He lifted a cupcake from the shelf and bit
only the icing off its head.
Then with his blue-dyed mouth
said, *I don't eat the bread.*

In the beginning
one may make such declarations,
believe it possible to live on cloudy stuff
that floats over
a mother's cart, its half-price loaf.

Sometimes, Crystal would bring cake for lunch.

A decadent diet, I thought,
believing, then, in choice.

This was after weddings were called off
or expectations for a holiday were too high
that she'd come with only dessert.

She didn't share.

Sometimes, she didn't bring a thing.

❧

When my mother wasn't watching,
my grandfather used to pour
syrup on my pancakes, in proportions
he saw fitting, flooding the plate.
I drank from the lip.

The maple was artificial, I'm sure.
But the feelings in me were real—

and the realization
afterward, of excess, sickening.

❧

If there was cakewalk including every kind,
when the music stopped,

some would be in the position
to receive layers overrun with ganache and filled
with cream between, a three-tiered tower,
or a torte topped with fondant flowers.

Some would find themselves stuck
at milkless cake, eggless cake, or butterless—
a cake defined by what it lacks.

—

Somebody sent a stack cake
to the school. A country recipe,
cooked over wood, in cast iron, soused
with sorghum—unrefined sweetener
poor families wrung from their own cane

once. Teachers praised the historicity,
but the kids knew it was ugly.

Nobody made the mistake
of bringing journey cake, a cornmeal round
hard as the travel it was made to bear
with the Shawnee, or some say Cherokee,
or some say the enslaved.
The origins are uncertain.

—

What I did not learn until twenty years after,
but is known for sure,

is that cakewalks come from plantations,
were performances slaves were forced
to put on, parading in front of their masters.

So how is it cakewalks were held at my school
and children were brought to them, happily?

—

So many things, you aren't told for a while.
Parents put candles on birthday cakes
for a while. No matter if wishes can be.

No matter the trailer from which a child may come,
to which classmates will have to go
if there is a party.

Trailer they make fun of for years after.
Your daddy fixed that door yet,
or did he bust it 'cause he likes to look at you?

———

Some kinds, you can't help,
my grandfather would say
when my mother gave me cans
for the food drive, coins for some raffle.

How harsh he used to talk
of others not light as white cake
and at least as rich.

How hard was his voice
and, if not the landing of his hand, his eyes

when my grandmother, busy with the wrong chore,
didn't keep his coffee cup refilled. He'd circle
his finger around the bottom, then lift it,
the dryness on display.

———

By 97, in his final year, he stayed quiet, mostly.
Or he complimented my mother and me.

We could not help but serve
the square cakes he preferred.

———

Crystal never attended a party.
Neither should she ride

with her daddy, she told the bus driver,
when his truck was waiting after school.

But she went somewhere with somebody.
I saw one *Missing* notice,
and never her again.

—❧—

My favorite birthday cake ever
was one that cracked.
I placed toy animals careening
into the crevasses,
called it earthquake cake.

It was run through with faults,
but I didn't know to see it that way.

That particular, special day, my mother
wanted me to have festivity,
and I did.

—❧—

Some cooks don't give up their endeavors,
though their good is of the smallest sort.

Crazy cake, depression cake, war cake—
these arose from food shortages
(no milk, no eggs, no butter),
as fortunes and bombs fell.

—❧—

We granted my grandfather
square cakes, understanding
maximum icing could be applied
to that shape.

And that the old tongue is untaught
tastes, becomes simple. Sweet is all
he could sense in the end,
palate turned back
to a boy's.

Which did not mean anything would ever be easy
for him again. Or hadn't been worse for others.

Just that gyms and the greater sites of competition
had, in the end, sent him back to a woman
in a kitchen. (Someone must feed both
a boy and an old man.)

My mother favors
tomato pie, pickles, turnip greens, lima beans,
succotash, slaw, squash fritters, likes to fix
enough vegetable sides to dominate plates.

But, for family occasions, she'll make
the effort of cakes. And so show
her greater hunger:

to give the world,
to cut for those most akin and close
to her, the slices thickest with caramel
from the four corners of it all.

Blackberries

Be reasonable: no spirit, bone, ghost business.
This is jam-making. That's a cloud of steam off the pot.

Your mother's teeth are blacked out
because she's been eating blackberries.

This is your last chance. This is the final summer picking.
Listen to her now, what she's trying to teach you.

Drop some of what you've cooked down on a cool plate.
Hope it sets up. It's a solid thing we're after here.

Cut the bone, count the circles inside,
to learn how long a dinosaur lived.
That's what a paleontologist does,

who knows it's fossil, not bone,
works in a field where *extinct*
and *extant* splits everything.

But two letters' difference
does not provide space enough
between for the gradations

of *lost* and *lingering.* The feeling
of *too late* that overstuffs the chests
of the living with ache.

Or the room-filling light
that animates a diamond ring
every time it is lifted from the box

where it has long lain,
though the person is buried
who gave it to me.

The mountain-building events of
our region prevented preservation
of remains, the scientist claims.

What we have to study of history
are only fossils washed downstream,
saved in sand, and by the sea.

Bloat and float is the name
of this theory. I would rather
speak of a buoyant body

carrying, over hundreds of miles,
millions of years, a story. And turn
my attention to the student

in the lab *rearticulating.*
Putting back together
a skeleton is what that means.

The mansion where *Gone with the Wind* was written sits up on blocks like a trailer, underpinnings exposed, like a trailer, trucked down a road, relocated from one county to another that also can't afford its restoration, a green curtain of vines drawing over the decay. What should stay?

Trailers will not biodegrade (though they depreciate), are left standing in place, the older ones with the new, accruing, spreading like the pines over the soil too exploited for any more cotton. Slash pines, trashy trees, you could call them. At least these are not plantations as they once were.

And skirts cover trailers' plumbing. Are they the structures with ugly foundations now? On the first property a family was allowed to own, the original trailer is circled by generations to follow, in growth rings of vinyl siding. It's a sight. To come to see. This, as scenery.

Considering Words Received, February 14

Opening is one term for what archaeologists do—
or have wanted done—to mounds built by ancient cultures.
Like Mann Valentine, amateur, private collector, who sent
his sons to the mountains of the South to acquire artifacts
in 1870. With their family money, and name suggestive
of hearts of crimson, proclamations of romantic feeling.

> It's February. The month, in 1828, when the Cherokee
> first put their language in print, publishing a constitution
> they had to write the year before, in order to defend their
> independence, in the country where their ancestors had
> always lived. The month, in this century, of walking aisles
> of embellished greeting cards, or out in leafless, cold dark.

Valentine's Meat Juice, medicine Mann patented, source
of his fortune, was a demonstration of love for his sick wife,
according to the *History with Testimonials* he self-published.
Which also tells of the liquid being made by *tearing asunder
muscular fibre,* and *adoption of judicious pressure, liberating
from the entire body all the constituents contained in it.*

> *Looting, violating.* That's other vocabulary for excavating
> the sites of past civilizations, for taking pottery fragments
> away—the lips of jugs, the body shards—to be displayed.
> Valentine's heirs did this near, but at least not in, my home
> county, where no one would answer their propositions of
> buying relics or give information on mounds' locations.

Now, signage directs the gazes of drivers-by over the river
to a mound, a curvaceousness of land subtler than a hill. Still,
much is beyond grasp of people such as me—in no part Cherokee.
The characters of their syllabary on placards crook, curl, evade
English grammar. And what has survived in mounds so far will
be left buried, at rest. Just down the road, at another mound,

today's archaeologists are passing sensing tools above—
not digging in or disturbing—the soil. Studying, more than
high structures leading men met atop, pits for storing sweet
potatoes, indicators of where houses had been. Houses were
the property of Cherokee women. And the quiet days in their
small shelters—these are the occasions I want to observe.

By which I mean celebrate. What is to stay unseen
here includes hearths, bowls, jars—that much is known,
can be detected. Such pieces of evidence are referred
to as *signatures*. As in sign of a claim placed, a truth
vouched for, a declaration to which all agreed. Means
by which a letter's writer, with firmness and flourish,
marks its closure.

Articulated, in Two Parts

1.

With a tongue, from her self

sprung, the cat bathes.

What more is there need for?

Songbirds are silenced when they enter

that mouth. It never opens to pronounce,

offer, any part of the purr to another.

2.

But now the cat is having to bend a paw into a proxy
to reach the eyes. She closes them, to imagine the stroke

isn't her own washing, is my interpretation. My mouth
I use to shape words. To make sound greater than itself,

stand for a meaning, serve as reference to some other thing.
I commit to a system of symbols, of utterances supposed

to be understood by speakers the same way. *Our shared tongue,*
I may call the language, a phrase recognized as figurative.

Even suggestive, betraying a desire to be coupled and held.
Oh, Love, I admit you

(no matter how the subject's been slunk around) are who
every bit of lexicon is intended for, all implication wed to.

The American Museum of the House Cat

Cats in hieroglyphics had jewelry, and women of Bast wore cats—
        bronze amulets in the shape of mothers nursing as many kittens
as children the family wished for. Now, how many civilizations and
        litters later, cats, sway-backed from the number of babies borne,
hung with the pendants of their own teats, stray near the American
        Museum of the House Cat. A room along a rural road where I grew up,
holding 10,000 images of cats: an Egyptian relic circa 1000 BC, a body,
        whiskers intact, smoked inside an English chimney in the 16th century,
pet food and cigarette packs, plastic clocks manufactured last year,

        all displayed indiscriminately. Collections, usually, are culled.
When there was an excess of kittens in ancient temples, they were
        mummified, sold to pilgrims. But proceeds from this museum, realm
of exception, go to a no-kill shelter. I buy a souvenir for my mother. She
        was once my guide, I'm the driver today. Our positions revolved around,
but we're both here. Later, it will be good to think back on how much remains
        here. Wheeled, Victorian felines, waiting with keys in, ready for winding,
to roll in circling pursuit, glass eyes' repetitions aglow. And the carousel—
        as its nine cats spin, surely the calliope recording plays and plays again.

In Another Waiting Room, for Further Testing

The beeches retain their red leaves. The lady
waiting in radiology holds, with her right hand,
a burgundy felt hat, in her burgundy-skirted lap.
In her left,

        a bra. Her blouse, surely matched too,
taken in a test or process she's long since passed
through. When it is my turn for cold tools to be
run over half my greased chest,

                I try to picture
we who lie here as nudes reclining to be painted.
Seminudes, our greater source of allure the single
breast each keeps

           protected beneath her arm. I gaze
at the ceiling, stickered with adhesive stars, distant
as eyes of the women I have not met today. Though
I think back to them.

           I called the lady a *lady* because
she, shoulders bent slightly, is my elder and looked
like the most upright among the kneelers at a church
where the gospel is devoutly loud.

              Or she didn't look,
rather gave a sense, as a church does to its visitors of
when silence is the condition to be kept and shared in.
We didn't look. I can't say

           whether one bra was black
and the other white, one newer, or sexier, or showing
heavier wear. Only that, if any were light-colored,
the straps were scrubbed clean.

             When dark removes
trees from view, branches rest a little, droop just a bit.
Yet by morning's arrival, they loft again toward sun.
Let the lady rise,

         as I will, from this exam table. Before
going up from basement level, entering afternoon glare,
she'll fasten clasps tight, smooth lumps away, tuck ends
safely beyond sight.

When Asked to Explain Her Cooking

—after the Foxfire interviews about Appalachian foodways

How do the children manage without
the mother? What she left

as a recipe for blackberry cobbler was just,
Blackberries, enough

for one cobbler. Butter and sugar to taste.
Biscuit dough, enough

for several biscuits. How do you know
what's sufficient

and when? *I work the crust pretty well,*
and cook her. I don't time.

I just know how done looks, how long is
long enough.

Her few spoken words, in transcription
conserved. As benediction

offered. Remember how she, who did not
count or level

cups or spoons, had to be satisfied to use
the better part

of the bag, a good handful, a hearty pour.
These were her measures.

In the Gem Mine Capital of the World

In the Gem Mine Capital of the World,
stands lined the roads, selling buckets of red dirt

for visitors to sift through, wash on screens,
sloshing and staining their fingers and clothes,
lifting out stones.

The town's title was repeated
by billboards every few feet of highway.

This was home, familiar to me.
So I passed by the superlative claim
without thought of distinction, or singularity.

The name meant nowhere else were there more
mines of this kind, inviting you to
bring a bag lunch, vending drinks and sunscreen.

Not that the land, or its miners' futures,
held much wealth.

Once, for a birthday party,
I mined a full morning and did not encounter
a single pebble that promised anything

(that had even slightly flattened sides—
the intimations of crystalline formations).

You could be sure of some glimmering result
only at the salted mines that mixed foreign rocks in.

It was all fraud. That's what someone thought.

Or, he got tired of sluices running into the river
(their muddy red), and seeing billboards.
Chainsawed the posts, hauled the signs off
one night, 30-some years ago.

He gave back the view of the mountains,
faceted with shifting cloud shadow. Outshining
the 50-foot pictures of pointed rubies,
pinging painted sparkles.

Which is not to say mines didn't offer something:

Hope. Like I had, witnessing
birthdays, girls turning ages I too was to reach,
unwrapping surprises with pleased shrieks.

Extending even to grown men,
such as the one who uncovered a bit of green
—not a 7 Up bottle, after all, but a 65-carat emerald
the size of the brooch of Catherine the Great.
The idea of greatness, brought in proximity to our lives.

And a $1,000 reward for information
on the billboards' vandalization.

No one has collected that money yet.
Told down which road, behind which barn,
with green briar vines overgrowing,
the planks and vinyl are still piled. No one

has been honest,
if telling is what that means.

When I was young and mining, the end
of afternoon and the party were drawing near,
and everybody had treasure
(or at least a mineral, uncut,
in which she could place belief),

everybody except me.
My friend's father, who'd been
shaking his head in sympathy,
brought our final pails.

In the handful I took from the top
was an enormous crystal, a polished
and unnatural blue. I was happy,
and that was true.

Those who will mine nothing but
earth that is unaltered and pure
have their virtues.

While others take part in the fakery
of salting mines so the flash
of a kid's smile can be guaranteed.
And are as right

as the sign cutter was,
setting his sights on high, un-excavated terrain.

I cannot say his name,
what makes a rock valuable,
and a jewel actual, or what the odds
of any search may be.

Leave some notions
(discoveries and riches remain)
buried in the mind.

There is no criminal
—what real fault?—
to find.

In Summer Before Drought

When I was measured for a wedding gown, my hips were less
than half the width of my shoulders. Their form and the fashion
of women hungering and honing bodies away could have been
a caution, about a future not to bring children into, or bearing
great weight. Soon wildfire would burn the field where friends
gathered in folding chairs and *party* could be assumed to mean
how people were divided. But, the day I was a bride, I pulled on
the strapless dress, trusting the fabric, for a time, to hold. It did,
through the evening when tents pitched for the occasion were lit
by fireflies' blazes. The sounds of the full river and my full skirt
as I passed over the fresh grass to give a promise of all the years
ahead whispered confirmations. I was told I was beautifully slim.
Slimness a measure in which we were happy to consider beauty.

When Leaves Won't Let Go

A few leaves, clinging
to a few oaks. Into winter. Why?

A few leaves, on the lower
limbs, of the younger trees:

A juvénile trait, sources explain.
As if to say, *They will learn.*

Leaves. What everything's going to do.

      Or, some foliage holds true
      to the branch. Even the deciduous

      may make reference to their origins,
      the evergreens, the first trees.

      Ecological pennants, the golden remnants
      are also called. Streamer, banner, fanfare

      for the occasion of a day that does not
      much differ from the one come before.

To pack a picnic is to know what must go
together. Salad needs

dressing. If there are boiled eggs, include
small packets of salt.

If there is wine, a corkscrew. If there is
hot tea, it will invite

use of a thermos, whose lid is a loyal cup,
holding tight.

Sandwiches too are tailored for holding,
by hands, their companions.

Each Sunday when I was a child, my mother
was sure to prepare

meals we could carry with us. And now I should
not feel without a guide,

proceeding from my own house. Remember
to add ice to the basket

in the morning, in anticipation of the pleasure
of the afternoon it is linked to.

Likely, to find the best shade tree for sitting,
you will keep saying, *Let's keep*

walking. This is not about getting to the end.
Though it's begun

with certainty that all you will have,
you must have already.

If One Says *Red*

—*after Josef Albers*

Red is the highest hue in the rainbow.
At dusk, it is the first shade lost to sight.
Light is shifty, I could conclude, like so many things.

‹———›

And when a man writes, recalling me at 17, in red, *a color
you wore well*, grammar set in the past—
is it the admiration or the tense that means more?

‹———›

Dark does fall, adds layers. Covers over.
But causes no fading. The rosy, the ruby pigments stay.
Isn't he still writing? I'm still dressing.

‹———›

As I will morning after morning, all the rest
of my life, each following only a night with he who
I have married. I do not write back. There is no need.

‹———›

The one who receives love may be different now;
it is not what I give that has changed. Here is the face
of my husband, waking, making a present of his eyes again.

‹———›

Red is also the first color seen every day.
Everyday, the same—I say this to speak
of the dawn, the fresh blaze rising.

If Once Dior Rouge 999 Was a Thing I Wore

If carmine washes, pales
from tapestry and canvas,
it exists still—the cochineal
         grit sunk in fibers. If threads
         ravel, fall, and are buried,
         it is there—in the soil.

Cochineal is powdered beetle
shells. Skeletons of their kind
have, for millennia, made red.
         In cosmetics spread glossy on
         the mouths of women young
         today, the dye's use continues.

I used to dress up. Remember, Love,
New Year's Eve, the zippered sheath?
Or, think how soon you zipped me free,
         how much cuts of clothes and lines in
         our faces have changed since. Also, please,
         say how little such surfaces matter to us.

Before cochineal is mixed with
boiling water or wax, oil or fat,
applied to other material, it is
         measurable itself. Dye is more
         than a verb, a fluid, passing tint.
         It is a noun, an actual thing.

So, if we've shared a bed years now,
and the linens wrinkled, and if our
possible child bled out—
         If my form, cradling its own organs,
         remained to scrub the sheets clean,
         and after, and is here yet—

I can put on that lipstick again, without
any dinner party to attend, to wear it off
down your skin. The color kissed away,
            something of mine, will enter your body.
            To wait until when we're swallowed
            by the dirt, for such togetherness then.

A Great Many Discoveries

The gold of daffodils is a rare ore encountered
      in the dark tangle of mountaintop laurel. Planted by
a woman who lived so long ago, her house doesn't
      remain. Now there is only a blooming outline of where
walls are no more, the welcome offered widened by time.
      And the box of shiny rocks I once buried will be made,
by the 30 years I have tried to remember their place,
      if not into rubies, a revelation when finally unearthed.
As a warm flannel shirt, stored on the shelf for a season,
      when unfolded in fall, turns quarters in its pocket
to treasure and surprise. This year, nearby, a crayfish
      the size of a lobster was identified. That large a creature
must have been previously seen. Just not documented,
      scientifically described. Such a great many discoveries
are unremarkable, or unremarked upon, and so
      able to be repeated again. Many warm days, someone
wades into water wondering about lives not their own,
      overturns, then returns, the firm roundness of a stone.

The cat comes. After weeks missing, after midnight,
at a long-legged run, as a white streak down the center
of the black road, a return—

Passing houses that have held cries of, *How could you?*
and addresses of answerless silences that follow,
through so many things unsaid, this chance given again.

Now I will feed his boniness at the table's head,
let need sleep in my own bed. As if
caring for a pet's few pounds could bring back

other bodies disappeared, or meant I had not
shied away in their unsightly trouble and age,
or they could see how I cried out to the missing:

Kitty. Hung posters, compared the hold of the heart
that remains to the hold of tape in the rain, and hung
more posters and repeated his name. And this one came.

From the trees above, his ears' higher perceptions
heard me, still trying. Or from culverts' underworlds.
In late hours, in vacant lots' viney unknowables,

in the constant companion that is air, let there
wait receivers for all who have more to say,
and amend, and are unchanging, and call.

Old Road

This is neither a last time nor a first.
  Curve after curve, the mountain road folds
the car into night and cliffsides, then
  lets it slide free. The road appears to aim
into rock, as if routing a return to strata's
  original crash, before accelerating the car
around corners. The headlights look snuffed out,
  then return, unfurling over the fields. The sight
of what has passed is absorbed by the blacks
  of the eyes of animals. Then, bright reflections
are flashed back. Someone is going home, or
  leaving. She was someone's child, and will be.

You Must Know

From leavings, you may learn the animals. Look for tracks
of bobcat in mud and dust. Droppings and, in them, details

of what fruit (the pits) or meat (the fur) was the fox's feast.
Flattened places in front of the berry bushes where a bear stood,

reaching. Burrow into which a beaver bowed. Path into brush
deer filed along, too slender for your feet to follow.

From far off, you recognize your family by their motions—
their walks, their talking gestures, even with backs turned.

Likewise with birds, you can see whether they are calm or fidgeting
on the branch without coming close enough to view markings,

then how the wings look in flight. You must know
things by their moving away. The waving emphasis expressed by

your husband's hands will stay (as long as he lifts them) the same,
after his first, young face has been furrowed and replaced.

Concentrate on the silhouette slipping into shadow,
all that can be glimpsed from your distance. Be glad

of the field guide, so named because it was the first book
among the bulky volumes of science with the intent:

May this be small enough to carry with you.

ACKNOWLEDGMENTS

Thanks to the following journals, anthologies, and projects, in which these poems first appeared:

"Suggesting," "Given Such Options": *Narrative Magazine*

"After Viewing an Antique Blanket from My Home State, I Make the Latest Bed": *North American Review*

"Night Vision": *Greensboro Review*

"All the Elizabeths": *Mississippi Review*

"Considering Words Received, February 14": *Cream City Review*

"The American Museum of the House Cat," "Old Road," "How We Celebrated": *The Cincinnati Review*

"Evolutionary Record": *Sugar House Review*

"Years, the Woods Felt Foreign Here": *The American Poetry Review*

"Stretch and Span": *Zone 3*

"Attraction," "Her Own": *The Common*

"Fossils Aren't Found in Appalachia": *Harpur Palate*

"Realizing": *Salamander*

"In the Gem Mine Capital of the World": *The Cortland Review*

"Blackberries": *The Southern Review*

"Nutmeg and Mace": *New England Review*

"Practice": *San Pedro River Review*

"Receipts," "Silences," "Cakewalk": *Town Creek Poetry*

"Collectors of Local Minerals Are Likelier to Find What They Seek": *The Art of Revising Poetry: 21 U.S. Poets on their Drafts, Craft, and Process*

"The Way Taken": *What Things Cost: An Anthology for the People*

"When Leaves Won't Let Go": Georgia Poetry in the Parks project

A special thanks goes to Bull City Press for publishing a number of these poems in earlier versions in the chapbook *In the Gem Mine Capital of the World*.

Thanks for making this book with me Paul Slovak, Allie Merola, Anna V. Q. Ross, Jessica Jacobs, Austin Segrest, Melissa Range, MRB Chelko, and Justin Gardiner. Thanks also, Justin, for making that last thirteen years of a good life with me—and for more to come.

Thanks for the support Miriam Clark, my colleagues and students at Auburn University, and so many poets who have been my companions, if present only in print.

Love to Aunt Sandi, an important Ervin and part of my memories too. And thanks for everything, Mother, including the home where I began, to which I returned to write many of these poems, and that I will never truly leave.

©PARKER J PFISTER

Rose McLarney's collections of poems are *Colorfast, Forage,* and *Its Day Being Gone* from Penguin Poets, as well as *The Always Broken Plates of Mountains,* published by Four Way Books. She is coeditor of *A Literary Field Guide to Southern Appalachia,* from University of Georgia Press, and the journal *Southern Humanities Review.* Rose has been awarded fellowships by MacDowell and Bread Loaf and Sewanee Writers' Conferences; served as Dartmouth Poet in Residence at the Frost Place; and is winner of the of the National Poetry Series, the Chaffin Award for Achievement in Appalachian Writing, and the Fellowship of Southern Writers' New Writing Award for Poetry, among other prizes. Her work has appeared in publications including *American Poetry Review, The Kenyon Review, The Southern Review, New England Review, Prairie Schooner, Orion,* and the *Oxford American.* Currently, she is professor of creative writing at Auburn University.

PENGUIN POETS

PHILLIS LEVIN
May Day
Mr. Memory & Other Poems

PATRICIA LOCKWOOD
Motherland Fatherland
  Homelandsexuals

WILLIAM LOGAN
Rift of Light

J. MICHAEL MARTINEZ
Museum of the Americas
Tarta Americana

ADRIAN MATEJKA
The Big Smoke
Map to the Stars
Mixology
Somebody Else Sold the World

AMBER McBRIDE
Thick with Trouble

MICHAEL McCLURE
Huge Dreams: San Francisco
  and Beat Poems

ROSE McLARNEY
Colorfast
Forage
Its Day Being Gone

DAVID MELTZER
David's Copy: The Selected
  Poems of David Meltzer

TERESA K. MILLER
Borderline Fortune

ROBERT MORGAN
Dark Energy
Terroir

CAROL MUSKE-DUKES
Blue Rose
An Octave Above Thunder:
  New and Selected Poems
Red Trousseau
Twin Cities

ALICE NOTLEY
Being Reflected Upon
Certain Magical Acts
Culture of One
The Descent of Alette
Disobedience
For the Ride
In the Pines
Mysteries of Small Houses

WILLIE PERDOMO
The Crazy Bunch
The Essential Hits of
  Shorty Bon Bon

DANIEL POPPICK
Fear of Description

LIA PURPURA
It Shouldn't Have Been
  Beautiful

LAWRENCE RAAB
The History of Forgetting
Visible Signs:
  New and Selected Poems

BARBARA RAS
The Last Skin
One Hidden Stuff

MICHAEL ROBBINS
Alien vs. Predator
The Second Sex
Walkman

PATTIANN ROGERS
Flickering
Generations
Holy Heathen Rhapsody
Quickening Fields
Wayfare

SAM SAX
Madness

ROBYN SCHIFF
Information Desk:
  An Epic
A Woman of Property

WILLIAM STOBB
Absentia
Nervous Systems

TRYFON TOLIDES
An Almost Pure Empty
  Walking

VINCENT TORO
Tertulia

PAUL TRAN
All the Flowers Kneeling

SARAH VAP
Viability

ANNE WALDMAN
Gossamurmur
Kill or Cure
Manatee/Humanity
Trickster Feminism

JAMES WELCH
Riding the Earthboy 40

PHILIP WHALEN
Overtime: Selected Poems

PHILLIP B. WILLIAMS
Mutiny

ROBERT WRIGLEY
Anatomy of Melancholy and
  Other Poems
Beautiful Country
Box
Earthly Meditations:
  New and Selected Poems
Lives of the Animals
Reign of Snakes
The True Account of Myself
  as a Bird

MARK YAKICH
The Importance of Peeling
  Potatoes in Ukraine
Spiritual Exercises
Unrelated Individuals Forming
  a Group Waiting to Cross